INTO PANDORA'S BOX

Khadj Rouf

©**Khadj Rouf 1991**

All rights reserved. No part of this publication may be reproduced, stored on a retrieval system, or transmitted in any form or by any means without prior permission of the author and the publisher.

First published in 1991 by

The Children's Society
Edward Rudolf House
Margery Street
London WC1X 0JL

A catalogue record for this book is available from the British Library.

ISBN 0-907324-56-8
Designed by Sarah Rawlings
Printed by Grange Press

For my mother

"...like Juno, you make me humble in your shadow"

Contents

Contents
Acknowledgements
Introduction

Chapter I — 1984
What is incest?
She's had it better
The easy way out
The last day
Love
Forbidden fruit
The feeling
Having a nice time?
Epitaph
The isolated
Like a bird
Every nightmare
There's no way of winning
Secrets
My father's commandments
Child that was me
In my father's land
To my mother
Alone
Rage

Chapter II — 1985
Tell me more
What could have been
Mirror image
Self destruction
Walking free
The untouchable
Now

Chapter III — 1989
Dedicated to the defence
For my father
For my mother
Screaming in between
Khadija

Acknowledgements

To say thank you for the helping hands of my Mum, who has stood by me and supported me in all that I have done.

To Anne, who has listened and advised, and shown me the value in depending on myself. I haven't forgotten the Girl's Group, nor Trish, who are all part of my healing.

I would also like to say a special thank you to Mary Jean Pritchard and Emma Davidson for all their support and advice in the publication of my work.

Introduction

This is a book about incest; about the sexual abuse of children. Although it is essentially about me, the feelings expressed here are common to many victims of childhood sexual abuse. That is why I think my work is helpful and should be heard. I am under no illusions about my poetic ability. If you are looking for poems that show technical brilliance you will be disappointed! These poems were not designed for that. They were never hung on a structural framework.

If you are looking to understand the effects of childhood sexual abuse then I believe that you will find something of value here. You may be a professional trying to understand the feelings of victims. You may be a victim or a survivor trying to make sense of your own experiences.

These poems came from inside my head and my heart and they came freely after years of being suffocated alive in a coffin of silence. They are an essence of myself. And I am startled to find that they are a testimony of the changes that have, over time, taken place in me.

I was abused by my Dad from when I was about six or seven years old until I was fifteen and a half, when I finally plucked up the courage to tell my Mum about what was happening.

I had always enjoyed creative writing at school but I had always written about butterflies and pretty sunsets. Never about me. Never about my abuse.

Someone suggested to me that I should try and write down my feelings. That it might do me some good.
I was feeling very confused; depressed, guilty and angry. I had too many emotions that I couldn't deal with and no coherent way to express them.

I found it difficult to say a lot of what I felt openly to people's faces — hardly surprising when I had been forced to split off from my emotions and to conform to the image of a compliant well mannered child.

I also found it difficult to trust people, so telling them about my incestuous abuse was not something that I felt I could do.
I did not want to be judged. I had been betrayed enough.

Putting pen to paper was very therapeutic for me. I became a prolific writer and although a lot of my poems were not very well written, they helped me to untie the knots in my head.
Victims need support to express themselves about what has happened to them, and to be able to grieve for what they have lost. But ultimately, you need to be able to live for yourself. And it is obvious that nobody can do that for you.
My poems helped me to heal myself, of which very little remained at that time.

The majority of my poems were written between 1984 and 1985 with a few poems following later. My style has changed over this time. I was only 15 when I wrote most of them. Now I'm 22.

Most of them are addressed to my Dad, in anger and sorrow.
There is a strong sense of injustice at what was done to me by him. Bewilderment at the senselessness of it all.
Some are addressed to professionals, especially towards those working in the judicial system, such as barristers and judges.
Two poems are written for my Mum, and some are directed at myself.

A lot of my work expresses my feelings immediately after the abuse. *She's had it better* is one of the first poems that I ever wrote. *The feeling* expresses the terrible guilt I felt because I believed my body had let me down; I had got a physical reaction from the abuse. I felt dirty because I believed that I had actively participated in the abuse.
I now know that this was not my fault.

Much of my writing expresses rage and depression. Writing helped me to work through these feelings. *Rage* was written at one of my lowest points.
The reason that so few poems have been written by me recently is

because I don't feel the need to write about these emotions now — they have passed beyond the stage of being my daily companions.
Don't misunderstand me. Survival is not a bed of roses.
That is because life is not a bed of roses either!
Each day should be taken on its own.
At least I see a future now.
When I was depressed and outraged, I was too paralysed to see beyond my own pain.

Other poems are directed at social workers, psychologists etc, who I feel need to be more aware of the complex emotions that affect victims of child abuse.
Issues such as guilt and anger may be neglected because the victim does not openly express them. That is because she or he may never have been allowed to express these feelings before. Professionals should make it their aim to believe in the children they want to help, so that these children can believe in themselves. Victims of abuse feel worthless enough as it is.
They need a helping hand, not patronising.
They need support but not to the point of dependence.

I feel very strongly about the two poems written to my Mum.
The earlier poem, *To my Mother*, was written in 1984, the year I told. This poem expresses feelings that were prevalent for me at the time. I felt angry that she hadn't seen my Dad for what he really was.
But then, how could she have done?
You don't expect the man you fall in love with and marry, to sexually abuse your children, do you?
And at that time, there was so little awareness about sexual abuse that there *wasn't* anything for her to see.
Incest didn't exist.
Many, many people were fooled by him. Not just her.
Frightening isn't it? You can't tell what a person is really like — even when you have known them for over twenty years.

To blame my Mum is to 'unblame' my Dad.

She didn't abuse me, he did.
She wasn't responsible. He was.

For my Mother was written in August 1989, and sums up how I feel about her now. I am angry that society constantly blames mothers for the abuse and that textbooks coolly declare that Mums are usually involved in the abuse by turning a blind eye to it; or she didn't have enough sex with him; or she will stay with her husband because he's the breadwinner; or she herself is the stereotypical poor mother, damaged irrevocably by her own abused childhood.
It is an insult to us as women.
It is an insult to me as a Survivor.

We have battled hard enough to rebuild our damaged bond. It didn't help that we also had to fight a world of intellectualised abuse, provided usually by the writings of men. Thankfully there is some change, but not enough.
More change is needed within the legal system. *Dedicated to the Defence* tries to highlight this, because I am tired of hearing of the atrocities that regularly occur against children in court rooms.
It is barbaric — we should defend our innocence. Not punish it.

Khadija and *Screaming in between* represent my own growing awareness of my identity. I am mixed race. My Mum is English. My Dad is a Bengali.

For a long time, I couldn't accept being mixed race because it meant acknowledging a part of him.
Now I feel positive about it. I know that my culture was not the reason for my abuse.
The colour of my skin was not the cause.
Childhood sexual abuse occurs everywhere.
The Black and Asian community is closed because of the racism that exists in Britain.
Things must change.
We need to protect children of all races, colours and creeds.

I am now in celebration of my race, and in celebration of my survival.

This is a book about incest. About the despair of childhood sexual abuse. You can never forget. You never 'get over it'.
But it is also a book about hope. You don't have to be a victim for evermore. You can do more than just cope.
It is possible to survive, *to live*.
The greatest gift that a victim of sexual abuse can have is the gift of 'self'. That is true survival; it is release from the wheel of fire and it is the achievement of a greater level of understanding.

Never forget that good things *can* come out of adversity.
Survival is an attainable goal.

Please, open the pages that follow, and see for yourself...

Khadj Rouf
July 1991

Chapter I

What is incest?

What is incest? How can I explain?
It's more than sex, it's a lot of pain,
It's anger and pain and heartache too,
It's times when you hate yourself through and through,
It's nightmares and hate and secrets and lies,
It's a web of questions, of 'if only's' and 'why's'.

It's times when you cry and times when you shout,
It's times when you want to know what it's all about,
It's times when you hate and I mean REALLY hate,
It's times when you need to communicate,
It's times when you're lonely and times when you see
It's hard to exist and it's hard to be.

It's times when you feel yourself going down and down,
In a whirlpool so strong you feel you can only drown,
It's times when you're looking for something that's gone,
And you feel you really need someone,
It's times when you want your childhood refound,
But it's not that way because it's the first time around.

It's times when you have to fight with yourself,
And talk yourself through, get yourself help,
It's times when distant is how you feel,
And others when it's too painful, too real.
Yeah, what is incest? I think I've explained,
It's innocence lost and wisdom gained.

She's had it better

Sitting in the park, I saw a girl with her dad,
She was laughing and playing,
The kind of trust and affection that I'd never had.
She's had it better, I thought with an ache,
She's had a childhood. Her dolls, her toys,
She trusts her dad and that's no mistake,
All the things I never could.

I've lost years of my life and I cry over it,
I was a kid and then suddenly I was old,
All those years I felt like a perfect shit,
When I think of it, it leaves me feeling cold.
She's had it better, I envy her that
I know it's not her fault, but then, it wasn't mine.
Bet she's never felt truly scared of her dad,
Bet she's never called him a bastard, a swine.

I guess it shocks you to hear what I say,
Makes you feel embarrassed,
Makes you want to turn away,
But don't because you've had it better too.
And my future depends on people like you,
Please try and do your best
I've already started
Started to conquer the barriers of incest.

The easy way out

I knew how to end it all.
   It was easy.
      Razors, pills, scissors, rope.
         I could take my pick. I nearly did.

I knew how to end it all.
   It was easy.
      Steal some money, catch a train.
         Go anywhere. I nearly did.

I knew how to end it all.
   It was easy.
      Poison him, stab him, drown him in his bath.
         I nearly did.

I knew how to end it all.
   But it wasn't easy.
      Open my mouth and say some words.
         Take it from there...
              ... I did.

The last day

Just like any other day at first,
Nothing much to say,
But the revelations that followed,
Occurred on the last day.

A feeling that wouldn't be subdued,
Something restless inside,
My soul had finally realised,
That I could no longer hide.

The distance that had come between,
The wall once unscaled,
The final cry for help brought me through,
So the jailor would be jailed.

Although, still afraid of the outcome,
I was prepared to pay,
For the risk I took for freedom,
When I told on that last day.

Love

Love, which is supposed to grow so much more,
But mine diminished into hate,
Love, for me locked every open door
Its horrors too painful to relate.

Love, which didn't need a reason why,
It could steal, cheat, abuse and lie.
Love, which can bring you to your knees,
Just by saying 'Be loyal to me'.

Forbidden fruit

They thrust the fruit into our mouths,
And push it back into our throats,
Yet, *they* expect us not to swallow,
But we must or we will choke.

They sweeten our lips with wine,
And we lick the taste away,
We know the pain that always follows,
Yet, *they* expect us to disobey.

We live in the pain of the pleasure,
Its taste more bitter than bile,
The ecstasy greater than we can express,
Yet, we know what it is to feel vile.

We know the fruit we swallow is rotten,
That the sweet wine will one day be spilt,
We know the peaks of burning desire...
And we know what it is to feel guilt.

The feeling

Something stirs within me,
I can no longer fight the feeling,
The woman has outgrown the child,
It is my will he is stealing.

My anguish makes me cry,
I hate *it* because *it* makes me feel weak,
I wish the woman would die,
And the child too, because she's too scared to speak.

The feeling reaches its end,
Appalled and disgusted I leave,
Again I have submitted,
Alone, I sit and grieve.

Having a nice time?

You used me, abused me but that wasn't as bad
As asking me if it was nice, did I enjoy it?
I *tried* to turn off and say 'This is rape!'
I tried not to give in but I had to submit.

You laughed, you smiled and I closed my eyes,
If I said the wrong thing you totally changed,
Always the same, I had no peace of mind,
You, nasty and hateful, like something deranged.

Why didn't you just use me and leave it at that?
Why did you have to increase my shame?
You taunted me and you made me give in,
So was that all part of your cruel game?

Epitaph

In a dead part of my soul,
That was forgotten long ago,
I have found a small grave,
Barren, untended, neglected.

The headstone is old, very old,
And corroded by acid tears,
The winds blow bitter and cold,
And the air is electric with fear.

Upon the mound a toy is sat,
A clue to the corpse's age,
And a moist spot where someone spat,
In a fit of adult rage.

Upon the stone, I read the line,
'A secret death brings no release,
This betrayed heart still bleeds on
And she may never rest in peace.'

And so who will cry for the child?
From whom I was torn long ago,
Did he or I spit on her grave?
'til she rests I may never know.

The isolated

Isolated by my fear
No mouth to vent my rage

No free hands so I can accuse
Always watched and abused

I am sexless and mute
Followed by the ever present eye

That always says;
I'll kill you if you tell so DON'T EVEN TRY.

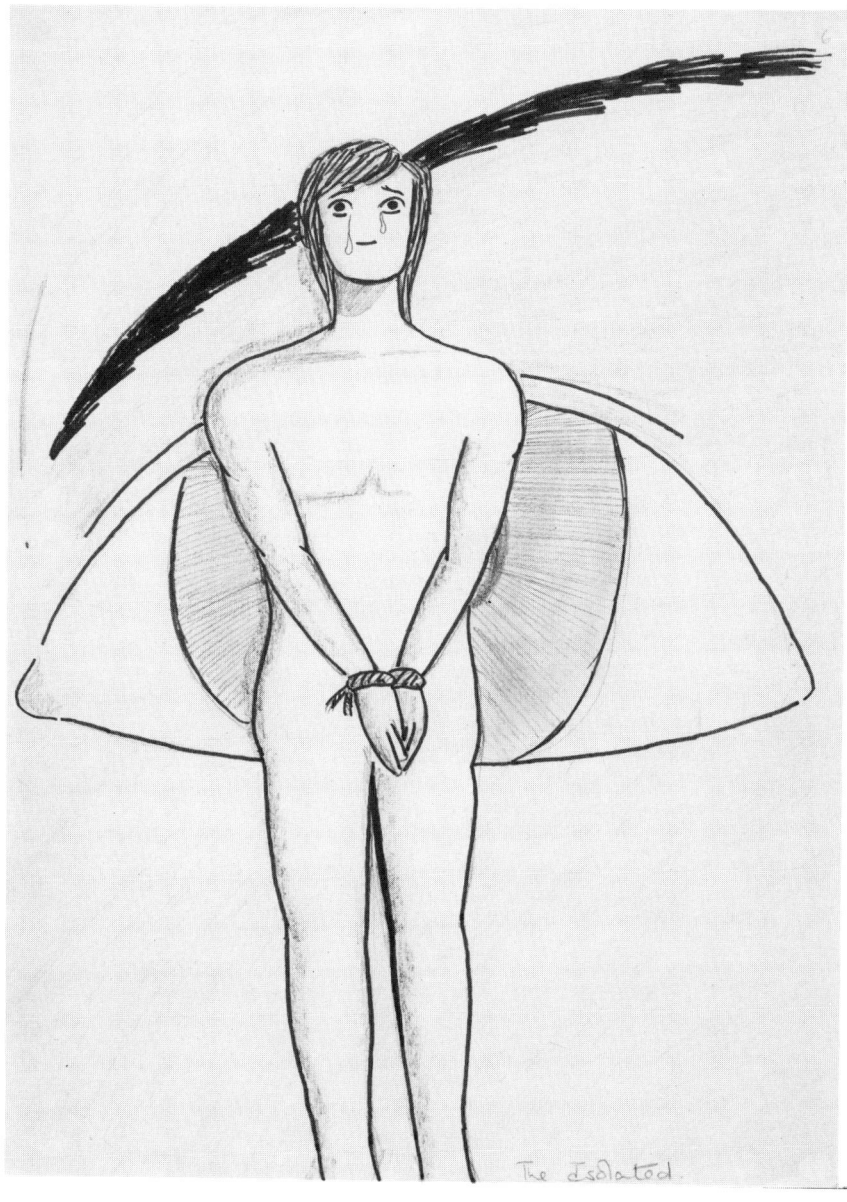

The Isolated

Like a bird

My weekends were filled with you,
And I couldn't get away,
Like a bird with a broken wing,
I *had* to stay.

Every night after school was a horror on its own,
You might be there when I got in,
And like a fly in a spider's web,
There was no way I could win.

When I was in the house alone,
I dreaded hearing your key in the door,
Like a lamb to the slaughter I lay still,
While you made me into your personal whore.

Every nightmare

In every dark corner where I won't tread,
Each shadow of my mind,
You taunt me, reminding me of your bed,
I look away in case it's you I find.

I hear you claw behind every locked door,
To which she holds the key,
You taunt me with the threat of more and more,
And I know that you want to destroy me.

With each insane glint of hate in your eyes,
With each stab of your knife,
I'm pushed closer to a cliff edge so high,
I know you're determined to end my life.

In every nightmare, I'm told to obey,
You like to make me scared —
Want me to rot in some maggot filled grave,
You know that no-one would have known or cared.

There's no way of winning

It is all over for you now.
What else is there to say?
The game has ended; finished.
You can get up and walk away.

With shattered pieces of my life,
I'm left standing here,
Now there's a new kind of danger,
I'm faced with a new kind of fear.

I'm scared of losing the battle,
And all that's left of me,
Almost too weary to struggle,
To search for my identity.

It is all over for you now,
No winner in this game,
You lost your right to freedom,
Now you, not I, carry the shame.

Although, I'm not Thurdsay's child,
I still have far to go,
There's no winning; just broken dreams,
I just thought I would let you know.

Secrets

Bonds made in blood
Secrets kept in shame
Tears shed alone
Yet, still I bear the pain.

Mumbling and talking in my sleep,
Fear in childhood dreams,
No-one sees the distress,
No-one hears the screams.

Carrying the burden,
Wondering why I was born,
Longing to be free and clean,
In secrets I am torn.

My father's commandments

'Learn, child, the things you are taught,
The world is against you and your kind,
Respect me for I am above you,
In this world, not one friend will you find.

Learn, child, that you are nothing,
Every law of God you have broken,
You deserve nothing more than you get.
These are my laws, for, I have spoken.'

1. Honour Thy Father.
2. Don't tell anyone about IT.
3. Believe that your mother is scum.
4. Do as you are told.
5. Make no problems for people.
6. Do well at school.
7. Don't speak about yourself.
8. Be well mannered to everyone.
9. People trick you. Don't trust them.
10. Never speak to men. They only want one thing.

Child that was me

Little child you had no defences
Into you, adult fears had not been instilled
And so sadly you didn't understand
That is why, little child you were killed

Little child you became the scapegoat
As always, the betrayer shunned the blame
You became like something diseased and dirty
Surrounded by lies, hate, guilt and shame

Child of doom, child of sorrow
Forced to lie and cheat
Kept away from a normal life
That is why, you died in a web of deceit

Little child I guess I loved you
But now you are lost to me
Even though you died tormented
At least I have your memory

In my father's land

His voice laid down the laws,
And so it came to be,
That in my father's land,
I could never be free.

His laws said, 'Don't be happy or laugh'
They said, 'Don't be sad or cry'.
In my father's land there was no way out.
I couldn't accept and I couldn't deny.

In my father's land there was always the agony,
Of taking the bitter with the sweet,
It was no use praying for tender mercies,
For the King's victim there was only total defeat.

To my mother

I love you very much mother,
And though it's hard to explain,
I have to know the reason
Why you never saw my pain.

Something moves within me,
The monster called Hate,
It points its fingers at him and then you,
You only saw when it was too late.

Oh, mother, you, the centre of my world,
Why didn't you see it was all pretend?
I will not hate you,
But why didn't you protect, defend?

You warned me of the strangers,
Who would rape a child without care,
I was never warned of the danger within my home,
And yet it was always there.

You never questioned the locked bedroom door,
Or the reason I was always depressed.
Seven days a week. I was never given peace
Think of all the sins I could have confessed.

I love you very much mother.
It has been hard to explain,
This has been Hell to put on paper,
But please, don't ever let him do it again.

Alone

I was surrounded by people but
                        I was always alone.
No-one knew what was inside my head,
              Locked away,
              Secret.
I was laughing but never happy.
                      I was crying tears of pain.
No-one knew me.
                      I was always walking free, but always
In chains.
       Restricting me.
                  Crushing me.
I never walked tall.
              I was always afraid.
   Alone.

Rage

Get off my case. Just leave me alone.
Knives cut. I'd like to cut me. Feel the pain.
It'd hurt. Tears. Pain. Sweat. Blood. Release.

Fuck. Piss. Shit. All the bad words.
I want to scream them all down the street. I want
to smash windows and spit on him, I want to
run where no-one can catch me, no-one not
ever, feel the wind on my face and in my hair, free.

Leave me alone mother. Leave me alone brothers.
Leave me alone sister. Nag at someone else.
Keep screaming at someone else. Not me.

I want to put my hand through a window.
My hand. The window. Nothing in between.
Just air. Hit at the window hard. Blood. Pain.
Splinters of glass. Release. I've done it. I've hurt myself.

I'm exploding. I'm going to splatter all over the walls
while people are walking past they don't see my
head's bursting there's blood coming out of my ears
my mouth and nose, my eyes are rotting inside
my skull.
No-one sees. All walking past. Grey people.
Empty people. I'm red. Always bloody red.

I'm going to cry and I don't want to. Tears.
Hate them. People sneer at you when you cry. People
laugh. Cry on my own. In the shadows.
Shadows don't give you away.

THE EIGHT FACES.

I'm imploding. Nothing is escaping. I don't speak I can't
drowning suffocating let go sink. Anger. Keep it inside
Sorrow. Keep it inside.

Screaming, screaming, screaming.
I feel insane I want to scream.
I hate and hate and what do I hate?
Who am I? What am I?
Let go. Let go. Please. I'm going to cry.

Can't get it out of me. Stab, stab, stab.
Please get off me. Filthy, dirty.
Scream. Where are the razors? Where are the people?

Locked doors. Stay still. Close my eyes.
I'm imploding. Hands, hands, hands.
Stabbed in the back. Stabbed in the front. Nag, nag.
I'm in Hell.

Stop. Dead.
Time to be nice. Time to be good.
Time to act like little girls should.
It's not nice to swear. It's not nice to lie.
Don't let the people see you cry.
Use your manners. Say 'Thank you' and 'Please'.
Don't let the people see you crash to your knees.
Don't go out. Stay at home. Be nice.
Remember, you can have everything or nothing.
But there's always a price.

Chapter II

Tell me more

Okay, okay. I've heard that before.
I shouldn't feel guilty, but I do,
I need reasons, answers, so tell me more,
If I knew then I'd tell you.

Okay, okay. I've been abused.
But what does that do to me?
Am I just a victim, a statistic?
Or an individual, am I me?

Okay, okay. It makes me feel sick.
That doesn't help me at all.
I want to know why it happened,
Why he did it to a kid so small?

Okay, okay. I won't tell a soul.
It's not talked about, I know.
What about my family — it's their problem too?
Will I ever forget, let go?

Okay, okay. I will be haunted,
But I need to get this out,
You haven't told me a bloody thing,
Tell me what *incest* is about!

Okay, okay. Go red, shy away.
Thought you were here to help *me*,
You're just like the others who stutter a lot
You don't care, as far as I can see.

Just because *it* has happened to me,
Does not make me some kind of shrink,
I am just as bewildered as you,
So tell me more and I'll tell you what I think.

What could have been

Tonight I feel lonely,
Tonight is empty inside,
Because tonight I cannot suppress,
The memories I try to hide.

I think of what I needed in you,
The starving unfulfilled
The sadness at what you could have been.
And all the dreams you killed.

The years that I lied for you,
Because I wanted to believe
That your word was true and you were right
And that I was the last person you'd deceive.

I longed for the hug that was meant for a child,
I dreamed of when the hurts would cease,
And all the while your hooks cut deeper into my heart.

Still I prayed for my release.

I feared your gaze, your every touch,
Your words cut through me like fire,
I wanted so much to be loyal to you.
I hung onto my dreams and became your liar.

I wanted to run to you with arms outstretched,
But your love turned out all wrong,
Sneers and taunts were all I got.
This is what I endured for so long.

I remember what I tried to give you,
And what I got in return,
I think of what could have been,
For that love I still yearn.

Remember me now as I walk away,
When you need me like I needed you then,
I'm clean of your 'love' now,
And I'll never trust you again.

Tonight I feel lonely,
Tonight is empty inside,
Because tonight I cannot suppress,
The memories I try to hide.

Mirror image

Mirror, mirror on the wall
Brings you to me when I call
Now that you're here we'll talk it all out
I will cry and you can shout.

Mirror, mirror when I feel a freak
I crawl to you all mild and meek
When he comes and splits my mind
I know in you a friend I'll find.

Mirror, mirror I held the knife,
He forced me to and I gave it life,
He stabbed me and I was filled with pain
Will you give me sense, make me sane?

Mirror, mirror go on yell,
Tell me that I'm damned to Hell,
Scream at me for all my sins
For keeping silent, for giving in.

Mirror, mirror I want to die
But I can't use the razor each time I try,
I look to you for consolation
And in return I get damnation.

Mirror, mirror I look at you and you at me
I wonder what the hell I see
A face that's hard, old and grey
But your face is like mine in every way.

Mirror, mirror that's it. No more.
Time to go back to the way I was before.
The nice little girl they always see
It's only you mirror, who really knows me.

Self destruction

I was one of God's damned,
And so I made myself enter Hell,
With my own special type of torture
I made myself pay for it well.

I bore my cross like a martyr,
And wore my crown of thorns,
I drank the bitter wine,
And my flesh was ripped and torn.

I tried and found myself guilty,
I became the People and turned away,
I condemned myself to death,
And left myself to rot and decay.

Yet, the neat corpse did not die,
And so I inflicted more pain,
I was the Judge, Jury and People,
And the Victim who only had 'myself to blame'.

Walking free

The flow of pain and unwanted pleasure,
The guilt of being me,
A sea of hope that's beyond all measure
And there's you, walking free.

Should you paint a landscape in my mind
With the greens and blue of dreams,
Then don't be shocked if you should find
Red blood running in the streams.

And should a figure beckon near,
Then do not be reviled
As her rotting face becomes clear,
The face of your butchered child.

You did once paint a landscape for me
But it all washed away,
The hills have turned into mountains
And now the colour is grey.

The flowers that should have been there
Turned into choking weeds,
But I shall forever watch you,
Dear father, walking free.

The untouchable

I am the smoke that you can see but can't touch,
I am the stars on high,
I am the ghost of memories past,
And I shall haunt you 'til you die.

I am the one who walked through the mists,
After the child had died,
Strong enough to live on after her,
I am the one who told and defied.

I am the music you don't understand,
The one who flies with wings,
I am the red glow before dawn,
So be wary of what the day brings.

I am the fire and the frost,
That once was your child,
I am the one you ensnared,
I, not you, was beguiled.

I am the flame that will burn you,
If you go too near,
I am the shadows in your mind,
Always present but never clear.

I am always with you,
Though you will never be sure,
Flesh dies but spirits live on.
And mine shall always haunt yours.

Now

Now I am lost
Now I'm confused
Now. Although I'm free
And no longer abused.

Now who am I?
Now where do I go from here?
Now I have been set free,
My future seems so unclear.

Now I'm unsure
Now, who am I supposed to be,
Now I have to relearn
And find an identity.

I am no longer the lesser, having grown,
And now I will follow my fate
I am no longer the death child,
That you cunningly chose to create.

I am the rain that stings your skin,
The wind that blows you cold,
I am the mind within the body,
Father, that you once controlled.

I am the things you can't touch
Yet, you plainly see
Try and catch me if you can
I know you shall not, for I am free.

Chapter III

Dedicated to the defence

They strut the corridors in costume
Pensive faces betray sweeping glints of arrogance
Regular performances echo in Houses of Justice
But empty Vessels make most noise.

Children's voices are drowned out
Hoping for justice, they are tortured in the witness box
Money buys safe disguises
And truth is conveniently forgotten.

Perfumed money deadens sense
'Everybody has to make a living', to rationalize duplicity
Tearful infants continue to stumble in legal mazes.
I ask myself 'Whatever happened to integrity?'

For my father

Are you happy to see me puking at my own body?
Nauseated by the only thing I could never possibly escape?
Are you delighted that at the point
When I am willing to give myself
His beautiful face
Turns into *your* face.

Are you joyed at the thought of my self butchering
And drowning in brightly coloured pills — prescription only?
Does it please you that my house
Once violated
Is now barred and bolted
To even welcome guests?

Do you relish the revulsion at my own nature?
The product of your own filthy handiwork
That you succeeded
Living proof, twisted and perverted beauty.
I draw back from passionate kisses
Frozen by remembrances of tasting poison.

For my mother

Do you know I look at you now we are at peace
And think how incredible it is
That we have survived the chaos, the blistering rage.
Wounded animals bite out at those nearest,
So it was with us.

The questions that begged answers from you
Once unaskable except in arguments,
Are resolved in my heart.
That we were both victims is clear in my mind
And I am satisfied that you never knew.

I know I spoke of it once with infant words
I'm sure if you had known how to listen you would have,
But the voice of the man you had married
Who made sacred vows of honour, love and life
Spoke with a stronger voice. Drowned me out.

I deny the text book descriptions of what we are
Written by those wishing to defuse the threat
Make us freaks, harmless; But are we as stupid as they would like us to be?
I refuse to let those complacent voices speak unabated
How often do they question *their* partners or the sanctity of their homes?

We have emerged, Mother, strong Women. Friends.
Despite their expectancies we are solid in our bond
Heart filled joy that we have survived the Janus,
Pain and sorrow that there has been injustice against you
Mother, like Juno, you make me humble in your shadow.

Screaming in between

On hearing a friend use the word 'nigger'.

You dare speak to me
Of 'it does not matter anymore'
When the word
Is washed with hatred.

You dare to smile
Pink lips, creamy skin
Belittling years of chains
Of lives stamped on.

You dare to ignore
My heritage, screaming in between,
Your narrowness mocking yourself.
You, my friend. A progressive thinker.

I could have cried.

Khadija

I want no part of you.
Don't want to acknowledge the life you breathed into me.
Don't want your breath, blood, smell or skin.
Scared to look in the mirror,
In case reminders of you are what I see.
Contamination.

You left me all in tatters,
Should I be blamed for wanting to cut you out,
Cut you out like a cancer.
All that was *you* that had touched me
Your words, commands, *your* religion, culture,
Your race.

With dry eyed compulsion
I butchered myself. I hid half of me away.
Cut my long black hair, renounced my faith,
Tried to deny the name you gave me. Nothing of you remained.

Nor myself either.

I swallowed tears,
A blood bond with half my family dissolved.
Untouchable. Unweddable. Liar.
These names replaced beloved grand-daughter, niece, cousin.
As part of me in a land of mango trees and jute
Exists only in memory. Ashes.

Here in my other home,
Through deep black eyes I saw hatred.
I listened to open hostility *and* the quiet comments
Of those who didn't realise that I wasn't quite one of them.

Half caste. Paki. Wog.
I was too ashamed to say a word.

But time cools rage until reason remains.
I have struggled alone for myself, for Me.
The name you gave me, strange, foreign
Is now mine. *Mine.* Beautiful and rare.
The name has been purged into my own
No longer belongs to the one who raped me:
You are not worthy of *my* name.

My family far away have cast me out.
I am not afraid,
I embrace, now, a greater family.
My cultures. *My* name. *My* blood. *My* race.
The paths of the sun from glittered gold to burnished bronze
Are living, fused in me.

I rejoice now in the speaking of my name,
Khadija.